M000043763

According to
punkin
sondra gray

TATE PUBLISHING, LLC

Published in the United States of America
by Tate Publishing, LLC
127 East Trade Center Terrace
Mustang, OK 73064
(888) 361–9473

ISBN: 1–5988643–6-X

Acknowledgments

This book is dedicated to Walter, my loving husband of forty-one years. The fact that he can occupy the cab of a big truck with me twenty-four hours a day, seven days a week for sometimes months on end is positive proof that he is a patient man. He is the one who gave me the idea for the book, and then he gave me the courage to continue it. I thank him from the bottom of my heart.

I also thank my three wonderful sons, Stan, David and Bentley, for the suggestions and encouragement they gave me.

I actually wrote the book for Ms. Rosie Ford's Talented and Gifted Class of 2001, Carman Trails School, Manchester, MO. They had a contest to choose a title for the book and made me select the winner. I thank them for their interest in the book, and a special thanks to Rosie.

My Aunt Delma let me know that she had no intention of giving up on me until she saw the book in print. Thanks, Delma.

Last but not least, except in size, is Punkin, who has been the best cat anyone could have. She has looked out for us across many miles. I hope you enjoy reading the book as much as I have enjoyed writing it.

Contents

Foreword

In thirty-five years of teaching, my students and I gained first-hand information from listening to guest speakers who actively participated in the workplace. However, our most delightful experience came when Sondra, Walter and Punkin Gray came rolling into our lives in 2001.

Most of us fail to understand the essential role truckers play in delivering goods that make our lives easier, healthier and more interesting. Virtually everything we buy has been transported by men and women who dedicate themselves to waiting patiently for their trucks to be loaded and then hurrying to stay on schedule so we are not inconvenienced or disappointed. They are also relentless in their dedication to keeping the roads safe for all of us.

When my students and I met the Gray family, I was teaching in St. Louis County. We were introduced to Walter and Sondra through a program called "Trucker Friends." The purpose of the project was to link truckers and students. The students would track the truckers' locations as they covered their itinerary.

Walter and Sondra had the creative idea of

sending each of my students a semiprecious stone or rock from locations on their route each month. Needless to say, the kids were highly motivated to identify the geographic location the stone or rock represented. The itinerary became real because of the physical evidence each child could hold in his/her hand. The kids loved receiving their shipments. The Grays even sent arrowheads to the kids one month. What fun!

The culminating activity of our program with Trucker Friends was to actually meet the Grays and to tour their trucks—they brought two! The kids were thrilled to sit in the driver's seat and have their pictures taken in the huge 18-wheelers. Another thrill was to listen to Sondra read the beginning of her book and to help choose its title.

Walter and Sondra know a lot about relating to children. They also know a lot about relating to animals. Sondra's story, told from Punkin's point of view, is filled with information about the lives of truckers and delivered in an interesting and poignant style which makes the reader want more!

Rose Marie Ford
Carman Trails Elementary School
Ballwin, Missouri

Chapter 1

Life On a Loading Dock

My name is Punkin Gray. I am a nine-year-old, blond, female Persian-mix cat with big gold eyes. Until I was about six months old, I lived in a packing house in California where oranges were packed and shipped. I can tell you that a packing house doesn't make a good home for a cat. There was barely enough food to keep me alive. As a matter of fact, I was so skinny that my ribs and my spine were easily visible. I stayed so dirty from living around all of the greasy machinery that I wouldn't even bathe myself. There wasn't even a comfortable place for me to sleep. Sometimes the people that worked there were mean to me, and I was afraid of them. My life was miserable, and in my "cat naps" I dreamed of having a home with people who loved me and would take good care of me and keep me safe. I wondered what it would be like to have a bowl of good cat food and a bowl of clean water that was all mine, and I could eat and drink any time I wanted to. I thought of how wonderful it would be to have a nice, soft, warm bed where I could sleep and know that no one would hit me or kick me.

One night while I was walking across the loading dock, I noticed a big truck pulling into the parking lot. A man was driving and a lady was riding with him. I knew the plan; I had seen it so many times before. I sat down and watched patiently as the truck circled the lot. The driver got out and walked to the back of the trailer and opened the doors, and then he got back into the truck and backed the trailer to the dock. The workers went to work loading the trailer with big boxes of oranges, but I had no idea where they would be going. I had heard the workers talking in the past about such places as New York and Alabama, and I wondered what these places would be like. Was it cold there, or was it hot most of the time like California? Were the people nice there? Were there large cities with crowded streets? Oh, there were so many questions about all of these strange places where that big truck might possibly be taking those oranges. I wished that I could sneak into that trailer, unnoticed, and find a new home, and new adventures.

Chapter 2

Cats Need Love Too

My mind had wandered off to strange places that I had no idea I would ever get to see, but my thoughts were interrupted when the truck driver walked around the corner. He looked like a kind man, and somehow I knew that I didn't have to be afraid of him. As we walked toward each other, my heart started racing wildly. He stopped in front of me, leaned forward and scratched me under the chin and called me a nice kitty. That was the first gesture of kindness I had ever known. I couldn't stop myself; I had to let him know how happy he had made me, but I wasn't quite sure how to go about it. I did the only thing I could think of. I curled my body around his legs, and talked to him with a pleading in my voice that I could only hope he would understand. I heard one of the workers say, "That cat needs a good home," and I desperately wished I could ask him to take me with him and give me a good home. He leaned forward again, and this time he picked me up and held me close to him. For the first time in my life, I experienced being held in gentle, loving arms. I knew that in a little while the truck would pull away from the dock and I would probably never see this kind stranger again, but for the moment he was my hero, and I intended to enjoy every glorious second of the time I had with him. If I only knew how to talk to him; if I could just think of some way to let him know what my life was like, and that the worker was right, I did need a good home. I really needed a good meal and some fresh water, but I didn't know how to say that. I did what came naturally; I rubbed my face against his shoulder and purred as loudly as I could, and hoped that he would understand what I was trying to tell him. Was there a chance that these people needed me as much as I needed them? Was it possible that they had missed having pets since they had been driving that truck? I was just sure from the way he held me and petted me that at some time he had owned some kind of pet. Maybe there was hope after all!

Chapter 3
Will the Lady Like Me?

The truck driver walked the full length of the dock, down the steps, and out into the parking lot, still carrying me in his arms. I wasn't afraid at all because we cats have a special sense about people. We can just tell right away if a person likes animals or if they are cruel. Even though it was dark outside, the lady saw us approaching the truck and let her window down. She couldn't see what the driver had in his arms, but she had asked him when they arrived if he would buy a bag of oranges for them to eat. She was happy when she thought he had remembered, but she was thrilled when he opened the door and set me, instead of a bag of oranges, inside the truck! She had the same gentle touch that the man had, and I knew immediately that she liked cats very much. She petted me, and talked to me as if I were a baby, and I loved it. She even fixed a toy on a string for us to play with, but all too soon the truck door opened, and I knew the driver had come to take me back to the loading dock. I tried really hard to keep from crying. I dreaded going back, but what I had to do now was find a way to show these people my appreciation for giving me the best few minutes of my life. I had been loved, petted, played with and even had the fun of seeing inside a big truck. The driver got up into the seat and sat down, and I couldn't believe what happened in the next few minutes. He asked the lady if she would like to have me. I knew I had a new home when she laughed with delight. "Well," he replied, "you had better hurry to that store across the street before it closes. She needs some food." Man, that was the best thing my little ears had ever heard!

These are the people that I came to know as my "mom and dad" and that big rig became my home. That was about ten years ago, and I have been fed, loved and cared for ever since. Of course I've made every effort to let them know that I love them, too, and I try really hard to "earn my Friskies."

Chapter 4

Never Say Scat to a Cat

Mom came back from the store shortly with dry cat food, canned cat food, and the cleanest water I had ever seen. She bought me a litter box and some litter, which I had never heard of, but I knew what it was for. She also bought a brush to clean me up with, which I didn't appreciate too much at the time, but I tolerated it just to please her. Before you could say "scat" I was off to a new life, and new adventures. I was not scared when the truck started moving, but I was just a bit startled when we went under street lights and they flashed inside the truck. I wasn't sure where they were coming from, so I jumped just the first few times, but I soon got accustomed to them. The weather was nice at first, but then it started raining, and as we went further north it got colder, and the rain turned to snow and ice. I could tell that dad was driving very cautiously, so I knew there were dangerous conditions. When mom started driving, I slept in the bunk with dad. I made sure that I was touching him at all times because I didn't want him to leave without me knowing it. Then we headed east and took that load of oranges to a cold storage warehouse in Ohio, where they put them into smaller trucks and took them to grocery stores. Our work on this load was finished.

So this is what the inside of a big truck looked like. I had seen so many come and go but had never seen inside one. What a surprise to find out there was a bed inside that thing. I found out soon that dad drives while mom sleeps, then they change places, and that way we can travel lots of miles in a week. Sometimes when we have extra time, we stop and all sleep at the same time. My favorite place to sleep is on top of mom's legs. There is a refrigerator with a freezer, and also a microwave so that they can eat in the truck when they want to, but its most important function is to fix my food when I want it warm. There is a TV and a VCR for when they have time to watch a movie, but I would rather sit on the dash and watch the big trucks go by.

I soon learned that by looking in the big mirrors beside the windows I could see all the way down the sides of the truck, all the way to the back corner, so I can keep watch while we are parked. I watch out for them when they stop for fuel. That job takes quite a while because our fuel tanks hold three hundred gallons. They usually take this time to clean the windows and mirrors and add oil if the truck needs it. I walk back and forth on the dash and watch whichever of them is fueling. If they stay out of my sight too long when they go inside to pay for the fuel, I go to the bunk and wake the other one.

One night mom was driving, and she had to stop to make a phone call. She walked into the darkness where I could no longer see her. I was so afraid that something might happen to her that I went to the bunk and *screamed* at dad until he woke up, then I went to the front seat and looked in the direction mom had gone so that he would know where to look for her. He went to see about her, and I was so relieved when they both came back to the truck. One time I got so upset because I felt the truck move when I knew it shouldn't have. Mom and dad were asleep, and I knew I had to do something. I tried to wake dad by screaming into his ear. That didn't work, and I was really getting scared, so I got my paw into his beard and gave a big tug! That'll work every time. Mom cautioned dad about getting out of the truck, so he got into the driver's seat, put the truck into gear and eased out on the clutch. When the truck started moving, thieves jumped out of the trailer and scattered everywhere. Mom and dad were so proud of me because I had watched the truck so carefully and let them know that something was wrong. That's when I earned my title as "Head of Security." This is the sort of thing I do to "earn my Friskies." Speaking of

Friskies, I think my bowl is calling. When I finish eating, I'll tell you about when mom and I got our own truck.

Chapter 5

Just Us Kittens

Because catnapping is my specialty, I have per-fected the art of keeping one ear on the alert while I sleep. One day while I was practicing my technique I overheard dad and mom talking about trading trucks. That woke me up! We didn't need a new truck! Why did we need a change when I was perfectly content with the truck we had? It was about three years old, and had about half a million miles on it, and it could start giving trouble just any day. It could possibly cause us to be stranded in a bad place, so I decided it couldn't hurt anything to look at new trucks. It might be fun. So, we went shopping. We found a nice teal-colored one, and I couldn't believe how big that thing was. The sleeper on a big truck is like a little room behind the front seats, and this truck had windows in the sleeper so I could sit in the back and look out while we went down the road. It even had a sofa that made into a bed, and a bunk above it that folded up against the wall. It had two closets, four cabinets and two large drawers. There was a large space under the sofa where I could snoop or hide. I thought it might be nice to have all of that extra space for storage and plenty room to play, but I sure hated to give up my first truck. As usual, dad made a really wise decision. He decided to buy the new one, and keep the old one, too. Now that'll work! He even had my name painted on the side. We drove the new truck and paid a driver to drive the old one for a while. That was a wonderful plan because he took really good care of our truck and kept it looking like new. Then one day the driver quit his job, and we had a problem. Mom and I decided we could drive it and let dad drive the new one. It took lots of sweet talking because dad said he would worry about his girls. We finally convinced him we would be fine, so we set out on our journey. Our first trip took us from Springfield, Missouri, to Hurricane, Utah, with a load of freight for Wal-Mart. It went to a distribution center, which is a huge warehouse that has everything in it that is sold in a Wal-Mart store. Every week each store orders the items it needs to restock from its distribution center and those items are loaded onto a Wal-Mart truck and taken to the store. Every large company has its own distribution centers. We took a load of motor oil on this trip. We followed dad as far as Flagstaff, Arizona where he went on west to California and we went north through the canyons very close to the Grand Canyon. In some places the highway was built right along the side of a canyon wall on one side, and we could look straight down into the canyon on the other side. The colors were such beautiful shades of red and orange, and when the sun started setting, the rock formations cast shadows of deep purple. It was one of the loveliest sights I have ever seen.

From there we went to American Falls, Idaho, and got a load of potatoes that we took to Greer, South Carolina. I found out while we were in Idaho that potatoes are one of their main crops. That was a really long trip, but we had fun. Mom knew how many miles it was, so she divided that by the number of days we had to get there, and that let her know how many miles we had to go every day in order to get there on time. Sometimes we have flat tires, really bad traffic jams, or some other situations that could cause us to be late, so she drove a few extra miles every day so just in case anything went wrong we would have some extra time. When she finished her driving time we would just spend the rest of the day cleaning and organizing our truck and playing. Mom was really careful to keep everything in its place because she didn't want anything to fall off the shelves and possibly hit me while we were going down the road. I really enjoyed our extra time. I did miss my dad though. I looked for him in every teal truck I saw, but I couldn't find him. Sometimes we were both sad, but we stayed so busy that we didn't have much time to think about it.

One day in early autumn we unloaded bicycle tires that we had taken to a company in Georgia that makes bicycles. Our dispatcher asked us to go to south Alabama and pick up a load of peanuts that were going to a candy company in Canada. I was so excited I could hardly wait, until mom told me I had to go to the vet and get immunization shots and papers so that I could cross the border. That really scared me because I don't like to go to a doctor, and I really don't like getting shots. I knew where we were when we got to the vet's office, and I trembled so hard, but I decided to be brave because it was just one little sting, and then it was finished. I suppose it was worth it because Canada was so beautiful.

We decided after about three months that we wanted to be back on dad's truck with him, so we got another driver for our truck, and later we sold it. We still miss it, but occasionally we see it going down the big road.

Chapter 6

Holidays

Christmas came very soon after we got back on the truck with dad. Since we wouldn't get to be home long enough to put up decorations for the holidays, we decided to decorate the truck. We put lighted snowmen on the front fenders. Mom put one of the snowmen's red top hats on me and made my picture. We made a very large wreath to put on the front. It had a big red bow, some gold balls, and two hundred little white lights on it. We made shadowboxes to go in the sleeper windows. One side had a Christmas tree with different colored lights and ornaments and the other side had an angel with lights around her. I had so much fun helping mom make them, except that I got all tangled up in the lights. She laughed so hard. She said I looked like a small walking Christmas tree. One day while she was working on one of the shadowboxes in the truck, she dropped a container that had glitter in it. Dad was sleeping peacefully until the container landed right on his head. Now that wasn't the worst part of the occurrence. That came when he got up and looked in the mirror and saw all of that glitter in his beard. Mom and I were hiding around the corner snickering until we realized how upset he was. The way it stuck to his beard, it might as well have had glue in it. Several days and several showers after that we could still see sparkles when the sunlight hit him just right. Mom decided to not use glitter on the truck anymore, but the shadowboxes were still worth the effort. Many times when we passed cars or went through towns we would see children pointing at the lights. It made us feel so good to know we had brought happiness to them. We decided that was so much fun that we would change them for every holiday. For Valentine's Day we put red lights in the shape of a heart and a bunch of red roses. For Easter, we put little white carts filled with spring flowers and bunnies in swings. When the truck moved, they swung back and forth. Across the top we added flowering branches with small Easter egg lights. In the other window we put a white cross and draped a red cloth around it. We put Easter lilies around the bottom and shined a black light on it. We were surprised at how many people really enjoyed it. Just before Halloween we put Jack-O-Lanterns with lights in them, and of course we added some black cats. Some of the best ones we have ever done were between holidays. We made one for each side. They looked like aquariums. They had aqua-colored backgrounds to look like water, with bubbles and seaweed going up the back.

We put sand in the bottom and treasure chests with pearls and gold coins spilling out of them. Then we suspended little plastic fish from wires so that they moved with the movement of the truck, and it looked as if they were swimming. We put lights around the inside so that they couldn't be seen, but they did light the inside of the aquariums. One guard at a warehouse where we were picking up a load actually wanted to know how we kept the water inside them. We had a hard time convincing him that they didn't have water in them.

Our truck, trailer and the freight inside the trailer is only allowed to weigh eighty thousand pounds. If we allow a shipper to load too much freight, causing us to weigh too much, we could have to pay a very high fine. Most states have weigh stations beside the highway that we are required to drive through. They sometimes check our paperwork to make sure everything is right. We were going west across Utah, through Salt Lake City and past the Great Salt Lake. When we got to the top of the hill, we looked back across the Bonneville Salt Flats, and it looked exactly like the earth was covered with snow, but it was actually salt. Then we came to the weigh station, and they had us stop. They kept us sitting on the scales so long that dad started to get worried. He was starting to wonder what they had found that was wrong or if we were overweight. When they asked him to pull to the side and stop he really got worried. They came out to the truck, and when we saw their faces, we knew there was nothing wrong. They were smiling. They only wanted to see our aquariums.

Chapter 7

To Groom or Not to Groom

I have never suffered such indignation! I screamed, howled and even hissed at my mom a couple of times, but nothing I did would change her mind. She was determined to give me a bath, so into that water I went with a splash, but she would not turn me loose. I'm sure I would have died of embarrassment if anyone had walked into the room. I was wet from head to toe, and as if water wasn't bad enough, she was spreading some slimy stuff on me that she called shampoo, and had the nerve to tell me it was gonna make me smell good! There's nothing wrong with the way I smell. I smell like a cat, for goodness sake. Then, the thing that really didn't make sense was that she poured more water on me to get the shampoo off. If it was gonna make me smell good, why didn't she leave it on me? Oh well, I hoped this humiliation wasn't going to last too much longer because she was reaching for a towel. Now that turned out to be even worse. She wrapped me up like some kind of baby, and talked baby talk to me. That was almost comforting, if only I had known no one would walk into the room, but that was too easy. I heard the front door close, then I heard boots walking across the floor, and I knew my worst fears had come true. It was dad, of all people. I surely didn't want him to see me in this horrible condition. As mom turned to talk to him, I got a glimpse of myself in the mirror. I looked like a drowned rat! My fur was all wet and clung to me as if it had syrup in it. I was sure I would never be normal again. I was going to spend the remainder of my life looking like a wet noodle. Then mom turned me back around, and I got a look at dad's face. I wasn't quite sure what that look meant, but as soon as he spoke I figured it out. He chewed mom out really good, starting with, "What are you doing to my baby? I could hear her screaming all the way out in the yard. Don't ever give that cat another bath. She will do her own bathing." Oh happy day! Saved by the daddy! That's the last bath I've ever had, except for the ones I give myself. I'm really quite good at it and it's something I do several times a day. I always bathe after I eat, which is very often. Mom did ask the vet about it, and he said that a cat is quite capable of keeping herself very clean, so baths are not at all necessary. As soon as dad left the room, she got out the scissors. This looked really bad, but she said she just needed to trim the matted places out of my fur. I was really glad when she finished that job. It didn't hurt at all, but I didn't like it.

Please don't misunderstand me, I love my mom very much, but I surely was glad to win that battle. But that was only one battle of a continuing war. The next trauma was getting the claws clipped. I have what they call a scratching post, but sometimes I use the nearest piece of furniture to pull the old sheaths off my claws. I stretch up as tall as I can, dig my claws in and pull really hard, and that does the trick. When mom catches me using the furniture, she gets really angry with me. Sometimes the furniture tears, so I guess that's why she yells at me, and still thinks my claws need trimming. I guess she's right. I just don't want her to know it.

Another thing I don't understand about all of this grooming is getting my ears cleaned out. Why does it matter if my ears are a little dirty? Nobody should be looking inside my ears anyhow. It's not like my face being dirty. My ears are my private property, and I sure don't like a cotton swab being stuck into them. Cotton swabs were intended for cleaning around the little, hard-to-get-to places on the dash of a big truck, not for cat ears, so please, spare me the indignity.

You know, now that it's over, I suppose the grooming wasn't so bad after all. Mom has laid me in my basket and covered me with a nice, warm, fluffy towel that she just took out of the dryer, and I'm getting really sleepy. I think I can take a very long nap now. When I wake, I'll tell you about some of my favorite toys. Good night.

Chapter 8
If I Only Had a Toy

It is my educated opinion that, for the most part, toys are a waste of money. I would much rather have the boxes they come in. A box has all kinds of possibilities. A good box can be a really neat castle, which automatically makes me a queen. I can just lie around in my castle all day and look pretty, or I can give orders to my subjects, which would be mom and dad. I can order food or have them play with me, or just whatever the queen wants. A box can also be a good hideout where I can hide from bad guys or big dogs, like my new sister, Phoenix, but that's another story. When I have a box in the truck, I sometimes pretend it's a ship. When the truck moves side to side or up and down over hills and around curves, it feels just like ocean waves. Sometimes I'm a pirate or sometimes I'm just taking a nice cruise on a huge ocean liner. But the most fun I have ever had with boxes was when mom put several together for me. She cut holes in the sides so I could go from one to the other just like rooms in a house. I could turn corners, and I could even go up one level, so boxes do make the best toys. Another thing that makes a good toy is a paper bag. They rattle a lot and make a delightful noise. When dad goes to the store to buy something, he asks them to put it in a large paper bag, and then he brings the bag for me to play with. I get inside it and mom runs her finger along the top and sides. When I see the shadow of her finger, I attack it. We always play like that until the bag is torn to shreds. Mom does still insist on buying toys for me, though. I get a new toy every Christmas and all through the year. I'm not sure just how many a hundred is, but I know I've had at least that many stuffed rats, birds, balls with bells in them, and other such things. One of the best ones was a bird on a long elastic string. Mom hung it from the top of the bunk in the truck and we named it "Fly-by-Night" because it just flies around all time. Sometimes dad gets in the bunk with me while mom drives, and we sit at each end of the bunk and bat Fly-by-Night back and forth to each other. That is so much fun.

Another one that I enjoy is a ball with a tail hanging out of it. I've never been sure just what kind of animal is in that ball, but it rolls around and I hide from it. When it gets close to me, I run out and attack it. Sometimes mom plays with me with just a piece of yarn or a shoestring, and I will play with her for a long time. I think my most special toy was a little stuffed doll that we called "Baby." Dad got him for me once when I was really sick. Mom and dad were so sad because they thought I was going to die. But I cuddled up to Baby and it really helped to have something to hold on to. It also let me know how much dad loves me, so I tried really hard, and got better. Within a few days I was back like my old self.

Chapter 9
Special Vets for Special Pets

One of the worst things that has ever happened to me was the time I mentioned earlier when I got really sick and mom and dad thought I was going to die. We lived in Springfield, Missouri, and mom and I were taking some time off the truck. Dad was picking up a load of mail in Memphis, Tennessee that was going to Florida. He called and wanted to know if mom and I would like to meet him and go with him. I was glad to hear that news because I was missing dad a lot. We packed some clothes for mom and some toys and food for me, got in the car and hit the road. Now since I'm a trucker, I like to take a road trip. It took us about five hours to get to Memphis but it didn't seem that long because mom talked to me a lot. A couple of times she gave me treats because she said I was being such a good kitty. Most of the time I just curled up on the seat beside her and slept. Before I realized it, we were with dad. Oh happy day! I was going for a trip in my big truck. We threw our things into the truck and were on our way to Florida, the sunshine state. The load of mail went to the airport in Tallahassee. We had a wonderful three days with dad, and then it was time to head back home. On the way back, I got really sick, and by the time we got home I couldn't even stand up. It was Sunday and my vet's office was closed. Mom was really scared, so she put me back in the car and carried me to the Emergency Veterinary Clinic. They did some tests on me, and then they gave me IV's and some shots and put me inside a little oxygen tent. Mom stayed for a long time, so I knew she was really scared. They made her leave that night. The phone rang several times during the night, and I could hear them talking about me, so I knew it was my mom calling to find out how I was doing. It seemed like a really long night because I was very sick and missed my mom. I worried about her, too, because I knew she was at home by herself, and I knew she was missing me. Early the next morning, she came and got me and took me to my vet's office. They checked me and said that they would like for mom to take me to the veterinary university where people learn to be doctors for sick animals. They called and made an appointment, and we were on our way. I was really scared now because I knew they would be doing more tests, but I also knew the tests were necessary for them to find out exactly what was wrong with me. That's the only way they would know what kind of medicine they should give me to make me well. I realized I had to be brave for mom's sake. I had heard mom and dad talk about doctors and hospitals for people and these doctors and nurses were exactly the same. I even heard them talking about a little dog that was one of their patients. They had put a pacemaker in his heart, and he was recovering very well. They were just as professional as if they were treating people. They even went out to the waiting room and had consultations with mom to let her know everything they were doing to me. Mom got a motel in town that night so she could be near me. When they finished the tests they were doing on me, they called mom and asked if she wanted to come get me that night or wait until the next morning. She was there before I could blink my eyes twice. We had to go back the next day, and they gave me several different kinds of medicine, and gave mom instructions on how to give it. Then they all petted me and told me what a good baby I had been, and told us bye. They had been so good to us that it was like saying goodbye to old friends. We went back home, and the next few days were miserable because of all that medicine I had to take. You wouldn't believe how much I hate to take a pill, but I tried to be a good girl. It was so much easier when dad got back home because mom would lay me on my back in her lap. I would always look to make sure dad was watching. When he would wave at me and tell me what a good girl I was, it gave me courage, and I would swallow it right down. One of the vets from the university even called our home to ask how I was doing. It wasn't many days until I felt like a different cat, and that toy dad got me really helped.

Chapter 10
What Breed is This Cat?

Early one morning while we were taking a few days at home, I awoke from a very peaceful nap to find myself eyeball-to-eyeball with the strangest looking cat I had ever seen. She was blond, just like me, but she had a long nose, long ears, and was about ten times as big as me. I suppose she just wanted to speak to me, but she didn't know how to meow. It came out sounding more like "woof." I wasn't sure what she had in mind, so I went on the defensive. I wasn't accustomed to strange cats coming into my home. I brought out what must have looked to her like forty eight blades, all sharpened and ready to do business. It was cat carving time. I had to show her right then who the recliner belonged to. I had already made it clear to dad, so she wouldn't be a problem. Before I had a chance to show her what a real cat can do, mom walked through the door, and I could tell by the look on her face that playtime was over. I was gonna have to hold that thought. She picked me up, sat down, laid me in her lap and started scratching me under the chin. I knew right then that I was going to hear something I didn't like. "Punkin," she began in that mellow tone of voice that let me know it was even worse than I had feared. "This is our new dog, Phoenix, and she is going to live with us and be like your sister." She's gonna do what? No way! That just couldn't happen. Neither the house nor the truck was big enough for me and that dog. What were mom and dad thinking? Well, one thing was sure; she wouldn't last long, I would make sure of that. As soon as mom left the room, I went to work on a plan. I walked right up to Phoenix and stared her right in the eyes, then I gave her a right hook that I was sure would flatten her, but she just turned and walked away. Now that didn't go like I had planned. What went wrong? I decided to wait a few days and try it again with a little more punch, but that time she saw it coming and just turned her head to the side so I wouldn't get her on the snout. Well, I had to give her one point: she was smart. I knew I would have to keep a close eye on her. I couldn't just allow her to move into my home and take over. She might eat my food and drink my water. Even worse than that, she might tear up my toys. I was convinced my happy life had come to an end. What were they thinking? I watched her very closely for the next few days. Of course, she watched me, too. She wasn't too fond of the idea of another right hook. Maybe I had been a bit too aggressive. She never bothered me when I walked past her. She had brought some pretty neat toys with her that she didn't even mind me playing with. Some of her food smelled delicious, and I couldn't believe it when she let me taste it. It didn't take very long for me to figure out that Phoenix is one of the best things that has ever happened to me. Of course she goes on the truck with us now, and I don't worry at all when mom and dad are out of the truck because I know she isn't going to let anything harm me. She's a real friend, and she watches out for me when we go on walks together. Sometimes when she's lying on the floor I walk all the way up her side just for fun. She doesn't mind; I'm her little sister. And if I need to get to some place that's too high for me to jump, she lets me use her for a step. She's really nice to cuddle up to when it's cold. I just lie with my back against her stomach, and lay my head across her legs, and we take long naps like that. One day a friend came to see us and brought his dog with him. She is a Shepherd Husky and her name is Cheyenne. She is so beautiful, and can run like the wind. She isn't quite as big as Phoenix, who is Shepherd Lab. They ran and played in the yard all afternoon. I sat in the window and thought how wonderful it was for her to have a good friend to play with for a while. They have become very good friends, and she visits often. Phoenix is always glad to see her. Yeah, I couldn't have asked for a better sister than Phoenix. She's the best!

Chapter 11

Dedicated to the Job

We were on one run for six months. They call that a dedicated run because that's all we did during that time. We hauled Federal Express, which is mail that has to be delivered overnight. We took it from Hartford, Connecticut to Columbus, Ohio, and then we went back to Hartford again. It was lots of fun because we worked very hard during the week, but we had weekends and every other night off in Hartford. It was too far to go home on our off days, so mom and dad decided to get an efficiency apartment so that we didn't have to spend all of our time in the truck. At first I didn't like the idea because I'm not really fond of change. After I had time to think about it I decided it was a wonderful plan. That would give me plenty room to run and play and new places to hide. It would be like having a new home for a while, so that was a pretty good idea we had. We found an apartment, I let them know where I wanted my litter box and my food and water bowls, and so far as I was concerned we were all settled in. Mom really enjoyed cooking meals, baking and doing her crafts, and dad's favorite things were watching television and sleeping.

The route we ran took us across Pennsylvania, through Punxsutawney, the home of Phil, the famous groundhog. I looked for him every time we went through there, but I never saw him. I was just sure I would see him on Groundhog Day. That's the day he is supposed to come out and let us know if there will be six more weeks of winter weather. If you ask me, I think they are putting too much responsibility on that little fellow. After all, what does he know about winter?

One of the best things about that run was getting to see nature's beautiful landscapes. Going the same route every day gave us a good chance to compare the different seasons. When we first started it the trees were full of autumn leaves, and the colors were so gorgeous. Mom made lots of pictures and put them into a scrapbook so we could always remember how beautiful they were. In just a few weeks they had all fallen, and the trees were covered with snow. I liked the way the snow just piled up on those bare tree limbs. Then there was an ice storm, and everything looked like a winter wonderland. When the sun came out and shined on the ice it sparkled so brightly that it looked as if the earth had been sprinkled with diamonds. Before we finished our dedicated run, the ice and snow had all melted away and it was the beginning of spring. The trees were starting to bud, and some of the wildflowers had started blooming. It was amazing to think about what it all looked like just a few short weeks before.

Occasionally we would go to the airport early so we could watch the airplanes take off and land. I always wondered where they were going or where they had come from. One day while we were watching, one of the pilots walked up and started talking to us. He petted me, and told us that he had three cats at home. He asked if we would like to see inside the jumbo jet he was going to fly that night, and of course we were all very excited. We had to go up lots of steps to get inside it. He took us up to the cockpit where he sits when he's flying. When I looked out the window I couldn't believe how high we were. I could look down at the tops of the buildings. I thought our truck had lots of switches and gauges on the dash, but it is nothing compared to that jet. I don't know how he can remember what they are all for. He gave us lots of interesting information about jets that we didn't know. Mom and dad thanked him for the grand tour, and then he had to pet me once more before we left. I still think about him from time to time and wonder if he is on the ground or in the sky.

One day when we got to the airport in Columbus we noticed something that we hadn't seen there before. It was the Goodyear blimp. That thing was really huge. We didn't get to go inside, but I sure wish we could have. We did get close enough for mom to get some good pictures. Making pictures is one of her favorite things to do. One day several months later we saw it circling Houston, Texas.

We were all really sad when our dedicated run ended and we had to move out of our little apartment. We had enjoyed it all very much, but we knew that with a little bit of luck we could do it again some day.

Chapter 12
Breakdown

Gloucester, Massachusetts, is a beautiful little fishing village not far out of Boston, just like the ones you read about in books. We had to go there to get a load of frozen fish. Mom said the place smelled terrible, but I thought it smelled wonderful. It made me so hungry that I had to eat a bite while dad went inside to get our paperwork. The streets go up and down steep hills, and the shops are built close together and very near the streets. From our vantage point we could see the Atlantic Ocean. There were fishing boats everywhere. The people were very friendly. Some of them waved at us when they walked down the sidewalk past us. Most of them smiled and seemed surprised to see a cat in a big truck. It was apparent that some of them were fishermen, because they had on galoshes and rain slickers. It was a different kind of place from anywhere I had ever been. We were there most of the day waiting for the workers to load the trailer, and I really enjoyed it.

While we waited, the temperature dropped and a few snowflakes started falling, but not enough to be visible on the ground. By late evening, they had is loaded and it was time for us to go. We got onto the street and moved through the traffic and onto the main highway. Now I'm no mechanic, but since I'm a cat I have very keen senses, and sometimes I detect a malfunction before dad or mom does. This was one of those times. The engine just didn't sound right, and it had a strange smell. Just then dad noticed that it was overheating, and he pulled to the shoulder of the highway and stopped. He turned on the flashing lights to let people know there was danger and got out to see if he could find what was wrong. He couldn't find anything, so he knew the truck would have to be taken to a shop and have a mechanic fix it. While he was checking it, a policewoman stopped to see if there was anything she could do to help. Dad told her we were going to have to get a wrecker to pull the truck to a shop. She left, but in just a few minutes she was back with large cups of hot chocolate for dad and mom. She even offered to take us to a motel, but dad said we needed to stay with the truck. The wrecker finally came and hooked to the truck. That was a scary ride for me. I had never imagined going down the road in the truck without someone driving it.

We finally made it to the shop and that was even more frightening. I have never seen so many fascinating tools or heard such strange noises. There was one really large thing that dad said was an air wrench.

It made such a terrible noise that I was sure it was going to get me. I tucked my tail between my legs and ran as fast as I could and hid under the sofa. Finally they told mom that she could bring me into the break room where it was warm, so we went inside. I have never been a lap cat, but that was one time I gladly stayed on mom's lap while dad talked to the mechanics. The ladies that worked in the office all came in to pet me and one of them even brought me some treats. I could tell that they all liked cats very much. The bad news was that it was going to take several days and lots of money to fix the truck, so we went to a motel. They were right.

We were there nine days and nights waiting for them to fix our truck, but we all got some good rest, and mom had time to do lots of crafts. I tried to help, but quickly found out when I stepped into her glue and walked through her beads that crafting is not my thing. I think those beads would have looked really nice if I could have got them around my neck instead of the bottom of my paws. Her yarn was another story. Of course I couldn't use her crochet hook, but I didn't need it. I have five hooks on each of my front paws. I tied it into some knots that she couldn't even untie. She got pretty upset with me, but I thought it looked really neat. I suppose I need a hobby other than crafting.

On the way out of Boston, we had to go through the Ted Williams Tunnel. There are chains hanging from the ceiling, and if they touch the top of a truck it sets off an alarm that lets the driver know his truck is too high to go through the tunnel. Guess what! All kind of bells started ringing. We were too tall to go through. A policeman came over and talked to us. Dad had a good idea. He said he could let the air out of the suspension and that would lower the truck. He did it, and it worked. We were able to go under the chains without touching. The tunnel was very neat. It was really long, but it had bright lights all the way through, so I wasn't scared.

After we got out of Boston, the truck was extremely dirty and greasy from being worked on. Dad decided to get it washed, so he pulled it into a large building. Now that was another experience. I felt like we had found Niagara Falls that I had heard so much about. That water poured all over our truck, and then they took large brushes on long handles and brushed the truck. Then they ran water all over it again to rinse it. It sounded like we were in a rain storm, but it looked pretty cool inside the truck with all of that water running down. It looked much better on the outside, too. It was really shiny after they dried and waxed it.

I need a nap now, but when I wake I'll tell you about one of my favorite hobbies.

Chapter 13

Call of the Wild

I've heard mom say several times that she wanted a little place out in the country somewhere she could sit on the porch and watch the deer play. Well, dad finally got her exactly what she wanted. I don't know what three acres means, but they said that's how big the yard is. There is a clearing in front with lots of trees in the back. We took our camper out there and set it up, and for now it's our home away from home, and we love it. I like to go on long walks in the woods with mom and Phoenix. Mom hung bird and squirrel feeders in the back yard. She put a shelf in the window so I can sit on it and watch all the little critters play. I think watching them is the best hobby anyone could ever have. Sometimes there are so many red birds, blue birds and squirrels that I can't even count them. One morning we heard a strange noise outside, and when we looked out the window there were two beautiful peacocks in the yard. We found out later that they belong to a neighbor that lives up the hill. He also has some goats, and they occasionally get out of their fence and come down into our yard. That doesn't make mom very happy because they eat her flowers and bushes, and if she leaves any clothes hanging outside, they eat them, too. We haven't seen them in our yard for a long time, so maybe he repaired the fences. We've seen several wild turkeys out there. One day mom didn't put the lid on the garbage can tight enough. We had just gone to sleep that night when Phoenix started barking and having a fit. Dad looked out to see what she was so upset about, and there were two 'possums in the garbage. Phoenix wanted to go out and play with them, but mom said that would not be a good idea. She also found a turtle ambling across the yard one day, and wanted to play with it, too. Mom caught her just in time. Phoenix wants to play with everything.

There are so many little hummingbirds around our house. We have counted as many as nine at one time. They are so much fun because they fly right up to the window and hover there and look in at us. That's how they let mom know when their feeders need more nectar in them. Mom and I wake up early every morning when we are home and just lay in bed and watch the squirrels jumping through the trees heading for their feeders. One morning mom was sitting beside the living room window and saw something through the corner of her eye. She called me to come quickly, and I knew by the tone of her voice that there was something unusual that she wanted me to see. She said they were quail. They looked just like six little brown balls with legs walking in a straight line through the edge of the woods. They stopped and ate some of the seed that the birds had knocked out of a feeder, then they walked on down into the woods. We still see them from time to time. There are rabbits everywhere. Sometimes they just sit in the back yard and eat grass. They know when we are watching them from the window because they look up at us, but they aren't afraid. They do run from Phoenix, though, when she's outside. She would never hurt one of them. She just wants to play, but they don't know that. I think the most exciting thing was when mom opened the curtains early on Christmas morning and there were three deer just a few feet from the window. Her dream had finally come true. They just stood and watched us for a long time, and then they walked back into the woods. We have seen them in the yard several times.

I really enjoy watching all of the little critters. I think of them as my little friends

Chapter 14
Fun in the Sun

Some trailers are called flat beds because they don't have sides on them. They are used mainly for hauling steel, building materials such as lumber, and anything that doesn't have to be enclosed. Tankers are just what their name implies, and they are used to haul any liquids from milk to gasoline. Dry vans are trailers with sides and a top, and they haul mostly products that must be kept dry, but don't have to be kept hot or cold. Reefers, or refrigerated units, are trailers that can be kept at temperatures from very warm to well below freezing.

We pull reefers, so that means we can haul ice cream or frozen meat in the summer time and keep it frozen, or we can haul medicine or anything that shouldn't freeze through a blizzard and keep it warm. We haul lots of fresh fruits and vegetables, so the next time you eat a salad or an apple, remember that Punkin might have been on the big truck that brought it to the store. We haul apples out of Washington state, and onions out of New Mexico.

A few weeks ago we had to pick up a load of lettuce in Marina, California. When we got there, it wasn't ready. The workers were still busy harvesting it in the fields, and it still had to be brought to the warehouse and put into boxes and stacked onto pallets. That meant we had until the next morning to do whatever we wanted to do. Mom had a brilliant idea! She said we were only a couple of miles from the ocean, so she suggested to dad that we go to the beach, and he was all for it. Oh happy day!

I had never been to the beach, but it sure sounded like fun. We stopped by a store and picked up some sandwiches and drinks, and some marshmallows to roast over a fire. I quickly checked my Friskies to make sure I had plenty, and we were on our way for a day of fun in the sun. We found a good parking place up high overlooking the Pacific Ocean. We got blankets out of the truck and all walked down to the water. Phoenix enjoyed running and chasing a ball, but I had more fun just sitting and watching the sea gulls and sandpipers. We saw dolphins jumping out of the water so high it looked almost as if they were flying. There were some good waves, and the surfers were taking advantage of them. One young boy had a remote-controlled wing, and we enjoyed watching him fly it. I think it would have been fun to chase, but dad said no. We stayed out there so long that I was really tired and ready to go back to my truck. We all ate while we watched the sun set over the ocean.

I've never seen anything more beautiful. Off in the distance we could see large ships. The sea gulls were still gliding around over the beach hoping to find a fish or a snail. Darkness was setting in, and most of the people had already gone home. It was so quiet and peaceful that we decided to spend the rest of the night right there. It had been a wonderful day.

We took that load of lettuce to Rhode Island. While we were going through New Jersey, mom woke me up just throwing things out of the cabinet. She was getting the camera out in a hurry, so I knew we were going to see something special. As we crossed the bay, she got so excited and started pointing and saying, "There she is!" I couldn't imagine who *she* was until I looked in the direction mom was pointing. There was the largest statue I had ever seen. It was a huge green lady, and I knew it had to be the Statue of Liberty that I had heard so much about. She was just as spectacular as I had imagined, and I was actually getting to see her. That night I dreamed about her. This had truly been an exciting trip.

Chapter 15

Pets, Pets Everywhere

Riding in a big truck is not at all like riding in a car. A big truck sits up so high that we can see so much more than we can from a car. If I want a really good view, I jump up on the dash, and then I can see everything. One night while mom was fueling the truck, I jumped up on the dash to see if anything exciting was going on. Besides, I knew she was going to clean the windshield, and it is fun to try to catch the brush. I saw something moving in the truck that was parked next to us. I couldn't believe my eyes. It was a big gray cat! It had never occurred to me that other trucks might have pets in them. Mom went over and talked with his mom and found out that he was very young. He had only been trucking for about eight months, so he still had a lot to learn. I knew that if he would try really hard, he could be almost as good at trucking as me. His name was Buffy, and he was very spoiled. I couldn't imagine a cat being spoiled. After all, mom and dad don't spoil me—well, they don't spoil me very much—well, they do spoil me pretty much. May we discuss this later? Anyhow, Buffy was beautiful, and I'm sure he will make a great trucker. I look for him when we stop for fuel, or when we are parked somewhere for a while. I really would like to know how he likes his job.

I have also noticed that we are not the only truck with a dog. Almost every time we stop at a truck stop, I see drivers walking their dogs. Some are fat, some skinny, some are big and some are small. There are all different breeds and colors, but the one thing they all have in common is that they all seem happy, so I suppose Phoenix is not the only dog that enjoys trucking.

We were parked at a truck stop one day in Ontario, California. Dad and mom were getting ready to go inside and eat lunch and take a shower when I saw a driver walking his cat on a leash. Dad said it was a cougar. I had never seen a cat that large in my life, except the time dad parked beside a tiger's cage. It was on display at the Tiger Truck Stop in southern Louisiana. That almost caused me to have a heart attack. When dad stopped the truck I came bouncing up into the front seat to see where we were, and found myself staring straight into the eyes of a Bengal tiger. I ducked down as fast as I could so he couldn't see me. After a few minutes I got the nerve to look out again. I laid my ears down and flattened my head as much as I could and eased up above the window ledge to see if he was gone. Oops! Still there. I wasn't taking any more chances. I got down in the floor and stayed there until we were a hundred miles down the road. Even then I was cautious about sticking my head up.

We saw one lady who had a Cockatoo on her truck and a man and lady who had a parrot. Mom asked him what his name was, and he said, "Cowboy." He could sing lots of songs, and danced while he sang. They gave dad one of his tail feathers to put in his hat band. We saw one man with a parakeet, and he could do several stunts. We've seen a few truckers with guinea pigs, and although I have never seen one, I've heard that some have snakes.

We were in Shawnee, Oklahoma, near Oklahoma City when we heard that several tornadoes had been spotted in the area. We decided it was time to park that truck. A really strong wind can blow even a loaded trailer over, and we didn't want to be on the road in those conditions. We parked at a shopping center, and just about the time dad set the brakes, a security guard came out and asked if mom and dad would like to go inside. They decided that since the truck was loaded heavy they would take their chances in it since they didn't want to leave me alone during the storm. That was before we got Phoenix, and they knew I would be frightened by myself. They thanked the guard, and he went on his way. In just a few minutes he was back. He said there was a tornado headed right at us and he really wished they would come inside. He said they were welcome to bring me, so mom grabbed my carrier, shoved me into it, and we were off to the storm shelter. He took us into a long, very wide hallway inside the mall. When we got inside, we were surprised to find out that I wasn't the only pet that was sheltered from that storm. There were other cats and several dogs in there. I think we all knew that it was an unusual circumstance, because there was no barking, hissing or spitting the entire time we were in there.

When we left the shelter, they let us walk back through the store. I can understand now why mom gets so excited about going shopping. There were so many cat toys, treats and other neat things for cats. Two of the ladies that worked there stopped mom and talked to her so they could pet me. Of course I liked that very much. I could have spent a whole day in that place, but dad said we had to go. We were so happy to see our truck sitting upright when we got outside, but we found out soon that there had been so much destruction all around us. There had been big rigs turned over and many homes and businesses destroyed. There had even been complete neighborhoods wiped out with nothing left except the streets and driveways. It was a day I will never forget. I often think of the people that lost everything they had that day and I feel so sad for them. I know how close we were, and I am so glad we were safe. I had never really thought about it until that day, but there are truly pets everywhere.

Chapter 16
Promise Me This

Boring, boring, boring! We had been home for eight days. What possible reason could we have for needing that much time at home? Three days maximum is all the time we need there. That's one day to do the laundry, one day to get the truck cleaned and ready to go again, one day to visit family and friends, then we should be back on the truck turning those wheels and getting the job done. But no, that wasn't good enough. They had to rest, dad had to go to the doctor, mom had to shop and they had to do all kind of unnecessary things, but I was ready to go. I'm sorry about my *cattitude* here but I needed to be on that truck working.

Well, I decided maybe they would be ready to go in a few days, so I might as well settle down and take it easy. At least I was ready to go as soon as they were ready. I have always followed mom around the house and watched her when she started getting ready to make sure she packed everything right. She always puts their clean clothes and everything that goes back into the truck into large containers. When I get too tired to follow her any more, I just get into one of those containers and take a nap there. That way I'm sure they won't leave without me. I had just jumped into one of the containers and was just about to settle in for a long nap when someone knocked on the door. I really wasn't in a mood for company. After all, I had just gotten comfortable, but I sure didn't want to miss anything. I opened one eye just a little. Mom opened the door, and right away I recognized the man and lady. They were some good friends who also drive a truck, and I had seen them several times. What I never had seen was that handsome young man she was holding in her arms. Purrrr!! Man, he was a looker, and he was looking at me with the bluest eyes I had ever seen. He had cream-colored fur with a brown face and tail, and was the fluffiest cat I had ever seen. Just seeing him made me blush a little bit, and I lowered my eyes so he wouldn't think I was staring at him. His mom told me his name was Promise, and I think that's the perfect name for a perfect gentleman. Even though he was the most handsome creature I had ever seen, I still hissed at him a few times just to make sure that he knew he was in my territory, and then I started flirting with him a little. I ran into the next room where I hid behind the sofa and peeked out at him. He came looking for me, and I pretended to be surprised when he found me. Mom got out some of my toys, and he liked one of the soft balls, probably because it had catnip in it. We played for a long time, and then we went to my food bowl. He sniffed my food, but he didn't eat any of it. He was thirsty, though, so he drank some of my water. I ate a few bites and drank some water. We had played so much we were both tired, so we decided to take a nap.

When we woke I was really disappointed to find out it was time for him to go home. After he left I couldn't get him off my mind. I think about him every day. That Christmas and every Christmas since, I get a card from Promise, so I know he loves me a lot. I think it makes dad really jealous. He said I am his girl, and if Promise doesn't stay away from me, he is going to cut his tail off right behind his ears. Of course I know dad would never hurt a cat. I have seen lots of good-looking guys, cats that is, but I have to say that the only one I really love is Promise.

Chapter 17

A Cat, a Rat and What's That?

Mom has always laughed at me because she says I don't know what to do with a rat. Now in my opinion, a rat has only one purpose, and that is to play with. The thought of eating a rat is simply revolting. The only things that go into this cat's mouth are cat food, treats, water and occasionally dad's big toe. It's so much fun to make him jump and yell when he's sleeping really well. But one little rat can be so entertaining. On the few occasions that I have been able to find one, I catch him, bring him out into the middle of the room, and sit and watch him until he runs. Then I chase him and do it again. Sometimes they get tired of running, and just sit and stare back at me. I suppose it's just a cat's nature to enjoy chasing rats, but when they get tired of running, they are of no more value to me, so I go on about my business, and let them go back to their little homes.

One night we spent the night with some very good friends. Since we were in a place that I was unaccustomed to, I was doing my usual cat snooping. I checked out every corner of every room. I even looked under all of the furniture, and on every shelf or table that I could jump onto. Mom and dad were going to make me be good, but I suppose the friends really liked cats, because they said it was fine for me to enjoy myself and just be a cat. I had almost finished my house inspection when I caught a glimpse of something darting across the floor. Playtime! Oh happy day! These people had rats! All right, I liked it here. I was gonna have fun tonight. It was the biggest rat I had ever seen. It was at least a foot long, but the poor little thing must have been as hungry as I was when dad found me, because it was the skinniest little thing. When it walked it looked really strange because it arched its back up very high, but it could run fast. That's just what I liked. That was a challenge. I was just about to take him on when the lady of the house caught me. What a party pooper! Most people would be glad for a cat to catch their rats, at least most cats. This lady acted as if she were protecting that rat. Then mom explained that this little fellow was not a rat, but a ferret, and he was a pet just like me. His name was Peanut. That explained his strange looks and the funny way he walked. He wasn't skinny; that was just the way he was shaped. He could get into the smallest places where he would hide from me, and then finally I would see his little nose sticking out. When he knew I had found him, he would run and hide somewhere else, and then after I found him it would be my turn to hide from him. We played for hours, and finally we were too tired to play any more. We curled up next to each other in the middle of the bed and went to sleep.

We both woke up early the next morning and started our games again. Peanut decided it would be fun to grab the end of my tail with his teeth. He had no idea it was going to hurt me. He was just playing. When he bit down, I let out a scream that woke my mom. She came running out of the bedroom just in time to see me circling the living room with Peanut airborne behind me still holding onto my tail. It wasn't one bit funny to me, but mom laughed so hard she held her sides. Peanut and I became very good friends and he has never bitten my tail again. Shortly after that, they got another ferret and named her Sadie. She became a good friend, too.

Chapter 18
Coyote Clever

For a long time after dad found me, I was very happy and playful until we would go back to California. Every time we went that direction, I thought they were taking me back to that loading dock. I was much happier once I realized that I belonged to them, and it was forever. We were on one of those trips and the truck was loaded as heavy as it could be legally. One thing that truck drivers are always concerned about is driving down steep mountains, especially with a heavy load. If anything goes wrong, and the air brakes fail, there are eighty thousand pounds pushing that big rig down the hill with no way to stop it. Mom was driving and we were going down Tehachapi Mountain, which is very steep and the road is curvy. Suddenly the truck started shaking so hard that the vibration woke dad. He commented that he didn't remember the road being so rough, and mom agreed that she didn't either. She was having a hard time steering because of the shaking. We found out a few minutes later that the road wasn't that rough. Instead, it was an earthquake just a few miles from us. We felt several aftershocks later that night. That was just a little too close for comfort.

The next day was a beautiful spring day. The sun was shining and there was a cool breeze blowing. We were in Los Angeles, California, picking up a load of playground equipment that we were taking to a new McDonalds that was being built in Detroit, Michigan. We had to wait most of the day for the workers to load it into the trailer. Mom and I walked to the back of the trailer to watch them. The warehouse was full of the unassembled equipment stacked onto pallets. A pallet is made of wooden boards that are nailed together into about a four-foot square. Freight is stacked onto the pallets, and then it can easily be loaded into a trailer. The workers get onto a forklift, which is almost like a small tractor with two long, flat blades on the front. They ride the forklift up to the pallet, slide the forks under the pallet and lift it up. Then they carry it into the trailer and stack them side by side until they have all of the freight that we need to take or until the trailer is full. They worked while we watched, then we decided to walk around in their parking lot. Out in the corner we found some of the equipment that had been assembled. Oh happy day!

This had to be the most fun place I had ever seen. Mom patted the edge and told me it was alright for me to jump up onto it. There were long red, blue and yellow tubes that I could crawl through and hide from mom. Some of them had windows where I could peek out to see where she was, and then I would run around the corner into another tube, or jump up into one that went higher. There was a large box full of balls, and when I tried to walk through them, I almost got lost. We played for what seemed like hours before dad told us they had the trailer loaded and we were ready to go. We jumped into the truck and were on the road again. We got onto the interstate and went east. We crossed the Mojave Desert and for miles and miles there was nothing but sand and cacti.

It was getting late into the afternoon, and I was starting to get sleepy when I heard dad say there had been a chemical spill, and we were going to have to backtrack. He said we would be going across Hoover Dam soon, so I made sure I stayed awake to see it. I jumped up onto the dash so that I would be sure to have a good view. It was certainly worth staying awake for, and I'm glad I did because big trucks can't go that way now. We went downhill and around hairpin curves to the left and to the right until we were on the dam. It was already night time when we got there, and the whole place was aglow with amber lights. We were almost surrounded by very high rock cliffs just like walls that went straight up. Just as we came off the dam and started up the other side and around the curves, in the blink of an eye something darted across the road in front of us. It moved so fast that I barely had time to see that it was a coyote. I wondered where he was going, but without any hesitation he went straight up that rock wall. I would never have dreamed that a coyote could climb a rock, but he did it, and I knew it wasn't the first time he had been up there. I couldn't keep from wondering what sort of adventures that little guy was going to have out there on that desert, but he didn't seem to be afraid. He had probably already made friends with all of the desert critters.

Chapter 19

Life of a Trucker

Next time you look at a trailer, try to guess how may M&Ms would be inside if it were filled from front to back, top to bottom with boxes full of packs of them. Sometimes we go to the candy factories where M&Ms are made. They also make several kinds of candy bars. We can smell the chocolate as soon as we drive into the parking lot. Occasionally they give us big bags of candy. Of course I can't eat any of it because cats are not supposed to eat chocolate, but mom and dad really enjoy it. They always give me some of my treats so that I won't feel left out. There are several different warehouses where those loads of candy might go, such as Kennesaw, Georgia or Waco, Texas. When we get there, we have to drop the loaded trailer. In order to do that we have to turn a handle that is under the edge of the trailer, and as we turn it, two legs come down under the front, and that's what it sits on when it is not attached to a truck. We call those legs the landing gear, and you can see them under the front of any trailer that doesn't have a truck in front of it. Then we disconnect the air lines which make the brakes work, and the electrical line which makes the lights work. Then we pull out from under the trailer, back under an empty trailer, hook up our lines, raise the landing gear, and go get our next load.

We had dropped a trailer load of candy in Denver, Colorado, and had to take the empty one to Dodge City, Kansas, to pick up a load of meat. We had to take half of that load to Buffalo, New York, and the other half went to Newark, New Jersey. It was really cold when we left Kansas, and by the time we got to Chicago, Illinois, it had started snowing very hard. Snow started piling up on the hood of the truck and around the edges of the windshield. Dad was driving, and I got up onto the dash so I could help him watch the road. I tried to catch the windshield wipers a few times. That is a really neat game, but I realized I should be still and not distract dad while we were in such danger. It was already night time and we could see amber lights flashing in the distance. It had already snowed so much that the lines in the highway were covered, and the only way we could tell where we were supposed to be was by the tracks that had been made by other trucks and cars in front of us. Snow had almost covered the tracks already, and I hoped we were making fresh tracks that would help the people behind us.

We were getting closer to the blinking lights

but I still didn't know what they were. Dad had slowed down a lot so that if the truck started sliding he would have a better chance of stopping it without sliding into the ditch or into another vehicle. A car passed us, and he must have been in a hurry because he was going much too fast for the conditions. I suppose he got scared, because he hit his brakes too hard. That was a big mistake. He started sliding and spinning around, and got sideways in the road right in front of us. Dad just held the truck as steady as he could. The little car hit the guard rail on the right and spun around in the other direction and came back in front of us again. Dad had to make a quick decision because he couldn't be sure which way the car would spin next. He moved very carefully into the left lane. The car slid to the right shoulder of the road and came to a stop. I hope he learned a very important lesson that night; when road conditions are bad, slow down and drive accordingly.

We had gotten close enough to the blinking lights now that I could see it was a salt truck. There was a plow on the front of the truck to remove the ice and snow from the road, and a spreader on the back that threw salt to help melt the new snow that fell. We call those trucks salt shakers. The only problem was that he was going the other direction and that didn't help us at all, but I was sure there would be some going our direction soon. The conditions continued to get worse during the night and dad decided it was time to park the truck. We know that getting a load of freight delivered on time is not as important as our safety. We finally found a parking place at a truck stop. Lots of other drivers had made the same decision dad had made because the parking lot was full of trucks. We were stranded there for three days before the weather cleared enough for us to go on. It was a good thing we had plenty of food with us because the truck stop ran out of food.

We made it safely to Buffalo, and by the time the workers had their part of the load off the trailer it had stopped snowing. We had just gotten out of town when I saw the strangest thing. I got up onto the dash again so I could get a better look, but I still couldn't tell what it was. It looked almost like a cloud, but it was coming up from the ground. When mom noticed me stretching my neck to see it, she looked to see what I was looking at. She got really excited, so I knew I had found something special. "Look," she told dad. "It's Niagara Falls!" What I had seen was the spray coming off the falls. I don't think I have ever seen so much water in one place, and it was falling down. That was the most beautiful thing I have ever seen. I truly wished we could stop and walk down to it, but we had a job to do. That happens to us so many times. We get so close to seeing something that many people travel for miles just to see, and we don't have time to stop, but our first priority is to deliver our load on time. That's the life of a trucker.

Telling you the story of my life on a big truck has been more fun than anything I have ever done. I sure hope you will watch for me out there on the highway. Remember that when you see a big rig, you never know what's in the trailer, and you can't even be sure what's in the truck. It just could be a *Punkin*.

Mom, Dad, and me
with my big truck.

I wear my own
kind of hat!

Now where is that
Bengal tiger?

Mom, I'm ready
to play, not nap!

Tate Publishing, LLC

Tate Publishing is committed to excellence in the publishing
industry. Our staff of highly trained professionals—editors, graphic
designers, and marketing personnel—work together to produce the
very finest book products available. The company reflects in every
aspect the philosophy established by the founders based on Psalms
68:11, "The Lord gave the word and great was the company of
those who published it."

If you would like further information, please call
1.888.361.9473
or visit our website at
www.tatepublishing.com

Tate Publishing LLC
127 E. Trade Center Terrace
Mustang, Oklahoma 73064 USA